S. Westray Battle

A Review of the Mountain Health Resorts of North Carolina, and Their Possibilities

S. Westray Battle

A Review of the Mountain Health Resorts of North Carolina, and Their Possibilities

ISBN/EAN: 9783337811204

Printed in Europe, USA, Canada, Australia, Japan

Cover: Foto ©Andreas Hilbeck / pixelio.de

More available books at **www.hansebooks.com**

A REVIEW

OF THE

MOUNTAIN HEALTH RESORTS OF NORTH CAROLINA AND THEIR POSSIBILITIES:

SUGGESTING THE DESIRABILITY OF GRADUATED SANITARIA OR HEALTH STATIONS AT DIFFERENT ELEVATIONS ON AND ABOUT THE ASHEVILLE PLATEAU.

SAMUEL WESTRAY BATTLE, M. D.,

P. A. SURGEON U. S. NAVY,

—OF—

ASHEVILLE, N. C.

A PAPER READ BEFORE THE COUNTY MEDICAL SOCIETY AT ASHEVILLE, JUNE 6, 1892.

ASHEVILLE, N. C.:
D. W. FURMAN, BOOK AND JOB PRINTER.
1892.

A REVIEW

Of the Mountain Health Resorts of North Carolina And Their Possibilities.

SUGGESTING THE DESIRABILITY OF GRADUATED SANITARIA OR
HEALTH STATIONS AT DIFFERENT ELEVATIONS ON
AND ABOUT THE ASHEVILLE PLATEAU.

THE object of this paper, Mr. Chairman, is to call the attention of this Society briefly to the unique advantage of climate offered by the mountain section of North Carolina. The merits of the Asheville plateau have deservedly become world-renowned, and it were ill becoming any of us, and, perhaps, more particularly the speaker, who has profited so much physically by a residence in this glorious section, though in the thick of an exacting practice the while, to utter a word that might be construed as detracting from Asheville's brilliant accomplishment. Still may she be set round with gems that go to heighten her own gorgeous beauty; and such I maintain is the case. From being a terra incognita yesterday, to-day we are attracting the attention of the world. From a mountain hamlet, we are a thriving, busy, progressive city, offering alike inducements to the capitalist and the globe-trotting health-seeker and tourist. But no one place can fill all the requirements or indications. Asheville is no longer the plateau, nor can it, in addition to its already admitted superiority, represent entirely, accurately, the merits of the higher table lands of the Blue Ridge and Great Smokies, which seem to offer in some instances Asheville's climatic influences, accentuated and intensified, approximating closely those of the parks of Colorado and the altitude resorts of Europe; for within a short radius of the Queen City of the plateau, an elevation, with attractions leaving nothing to be desired, of from 4,000 to 6,000 feet, may be enjoyed.

There can be hardly room for controversy that right here we are enjoying the golden mean of American climate. Medium altitude, dry, tonic, invigorating, ozoniferous atmosphere, which cannot fail to grow in popularity as meeting the indications in the cases of a large majority of health-seekers, more especially those looking for the all-the-year-round residence.

But when it does become necessary to advise a change to either a higher or lower elevation, let us not overlook the fact that we are closely surrounded with climatic conditions incident upon an altitude varying from 600 to 6,000 feet, at points yearly becoming more and more accessible.

But before going further in review of these inviting localities, let us recapitulate our own special advantages, which will serve as a guide in comparing the kindred influences which surround us.

What do we mean by the ASHEVILLE PLATEAU? What is the nature of its climate and WHAT ARE ITS MERITS?

1st. THE ASHEVILLE OR APPALACHIAN PLATEAU, with Asheville in its middle, is an elevated table land somewhat triangular in shape, embracing some six thousand square miles of Western North Carolina, with a general elevation of two thousand feet above the sea level, though there are points from one thousand to fifteen hundred feet higher just without the city limits.

It is upward of a hundred and fifty miles long with an average width of twenty-five miles. It lies west of the Blue Ridge and east of the Great Smoky Mountains, its surface being much cut up by cross-chains and spurs of its eastern and western barriers, as the Black Mountain from the Blue Ridge, the Balsam, the Cullowee and Nantahala from the Smokies. Hills, valleys, rivers and forests, so diversify this intra-montane expanse as to make it lovely and restful to the eye beyond the power of my pen to portray.

The great Appalachian chain, upon reaching North Carolina, stands sponsor to a section which should be, and I predict will be, the great sanitarium of our eastern country. As if conscious of its future importance it has seen fit to guard the plateau with its loftiest and grandest peaks, a half hundred of which tower to a height upward of six thousand feet, and a dozen pierce the sky at an altitude greater than that of Mount Washington, or any point east of the Rocky Mountains. As far as scenery goes, "age can not wither, nor custom stale its infinite variety," a point too little thought of in casting about for a suitable climate.

Asheville, the county seat of Buncombe, well situated 250 feet above the waters of the French Broad and Swannanoa rivers, and one mile from their confluence, is itself 2,350 feet above tide water. The entire region is covered with a luxuriant growth of primitive forest of pine, balsam and the handsomest of the deciduous variety of trees generally, the mountains being wooded to their very summits, an unusual and an attractive feature which delights the eye and at once impresses most favorably the tourist and health-seeker. The scenic effects to be had here are a proper food for the eye of the sick and the well, and in rounding up the complement of a health resort are not to be lost sight of. The Blue Ridge to the eastward is the water-shed of the mountain region of Western North Carolina, the plateau being well watered by clear mountain streams, the general direction of which is westward toward the Mississippi.

2d The CLIMATE OF THE PLATEAU. As Dr. Huntington Richards, to whom, by the by, in an article upon Asheville in the Reference Hand-Book of the Medical Sciences, I am indebted for many suggestions upon the subject of climate, justly remarks: "Any truly scientific classification of climate, definite in the value of its terms, and therefore capable of being exactly understood, does not up to the present time exist;" and, as he further suggests, it is to be hoped that an international congress will base a classification upon certain thermometric and hygrometric limits, and a choice of the leading meteorological factors going to make up a climate.

The climate of the Asheville plateau may be called a medium altitude, dry, all-the-year-round climate, enjoying peculiar advantages and many attractive features by reason of its geographical situation. It is cool in summer, yet the winters, shorn of their harshness by reason of its southern latitude, induce almost daily out-of-door exercise, in the way of shooting, riding, driving, or short mountain excursions on foot. Moderate altitude, dry and ozoniferous atmosphere, bright sunshine and beautiful scenic environment are the important factors of the region.

TEMPERATURE.

Observations extending through a period of eight years show as follows:

"Mean temperature of Spring,   53.49.
"   "   " Summer, 70.72.
"   "   " Autumn, 53.48.
"   "   " Winter, 38.87.
"   "   for the year, 54.14."

The statistics appended will compare favorably with any of the celebrated mountain health resorts in or out of the country. "During a period of eight years the mercury but twice rose above 88 degrees, and but three times fell below 3 degrees." "The diurnal ranges of the thermometer are very small when compared with the high regions of the west," the mean daily range being twice as great at Colorado Springs as at Asheville.

Dr. Herman Canfield, who has a handsome private institution for the treatment of chronic diseases near Bristol, R. I., spent some days here in January, 1886, casting about for a locality for cases needing special climatic influences. In a paper upon "Some Health Resorts of the South," the Doctor says of Asheville, "We have nothing like it east of the Rocky Mountains, and the resulting climate resembles closely that of the Parks of Colorado." And speaking of the PERCEPTION of heat and cold being a guide to climate, even more reliable than meteorological record, continues, "I traveled in the open air most of the time (January) without an overcoat. * * I did not feel the cold with the mercury at 32 degrees, in the rain, as I did at Aiken or Florida at 50 degrees with the sun shining."

HUMIDITY.

The mean relative humidity for the year at Asheville from observations of four years, 1876–1879, was 70.32 per cent., while the record at Davos, Switzerland, for 1876, according to Dr. Julius Hahn, was 75.05 per cent. Colorado Springs is dryer and would show a lower relative humidity.

Dr. Denison's Climatic Maps accentuate the fact that this region is the dryest in our eastern country. The mean relative humidity at Asheville for the winter from observations of thirteen years, was 68 per cent., while that of Aiken, S. C., for two years for the winter was 63.43 per cent; but Dr. Karl von Ruck, Director of the U. S. Signal Service Station at the Winyah Sanitarium, also Director of Winyah Sanitarium at Asheville, to whom I am indebted for the valuable tabulated observations here used, records the mean relative humidity, at this point as will be seen in the tables for 1888–1889, as 60.12, and for 1890–1891 as 63.40, making a mean for the two years of 61.76 per cent, thus verifying Dr. Denison's statistics.

WIND.

I have no means at hand to obtain data in regard to the prevailing winds. There is considerable air movement which is not an advantage to any resort, but there is less wind than in Colorado or any mountain resort in America.

ATMOSPHERIC PRESSURE.

The mercurial barometer registers usually in fair weather 27.55 inches. In altitude which is suggested by the diminished density of the atmosphere as shown by the barometer standing at 27.55 instead of about 30 at sea level, the plateau seems the golden mean, not high enough to disturb the great organ of the circulation, the heart, or the digestive system, yet sufficiently so to reap many of the benefits of altitude. The human frame is so constructed as not only to withstand a pressure of fifteen pounds to the square inch, or something like fourteen tons upon the whole body, but all the functions of the body are performed harmoniously and healthily under a weight that applied differently would forthwith reduce us to a jelly. It would be difficult to understand why any great reduction in the density of the atmosphere should not produce appreciable physiological effects, though, aside from those experienced by persons suddenly subjected to great alterations of pressure in mountain climbing or aërial ascents, the general effects of altitude have not received the attention they would seem to merit at the hands of the climato-therapeutist. Certain it is that man readily adapts himself to moderate alterations of atmospheric pressure, and populations of cities at an altitude as great as 10,000 feet seem to enjoy good health, and, so far as I know, show nothing remarkable in their mortality rate. Still, altitude alone, irrespective of humidity, and other conditions that may be associated with it, must affect the course of many chronic diseases, and I make little doubt that its influence in the climatic treatment of disease will be more and more appreciated as climatology assumes its proper place among the sciences. Dimnnition in atmospheric pressure quickens respiration and accelerates the heart's action; it increases the amount of watery evaporation from the skin and lungs, and diminishes the amount of urinary excretion.

RAINFALL.

The average annual rainfall is 40 inches, well distributed throughout the year, thus favoring agriculture and not subjecting the section to seasons of alternate rain and drought.

SUNSHINE AND CLOUDINESS.

The average number of sunny days (fair and clear days) from observations of two years (Dr. Gleittsmann's Tables) was 259 against 277 at Colorado Springs, the sunniest place in America; not a bad showing, certainly. It is interesting to note the fact that there is hardly a day in the year when the sun is obscured throughout the entire length of the day. The atmosphere being dry and somewhat attenuated offers little resistance to the solar rays which are peculiarly genial.

Dr. Gleittsmann, to whom we are indebted for the earlier data on the climate of Asheville, writes: "The temperature in winter (at Asheville) rises during mid-day, with few exceptions. to 50 degrees or over, and in sheltered places with southern exposure, where patients congregate, to 70 or 80 in the sun.

"The greater number of days in winter have clear, bright sunshine, and insolation being notorously more powerful in the highlands than in the lowlands makes out-of-door life all the more pleasant. The beauty of these bright, cloudless days, and their bracing and tonic influence on invalids, can only be realized by actual experience." My own personal observation corroborates the above figures and remarks.

3D. THE MERITS OF THE CLIMATE.

In regard to the merits of the climate, or the climatotherapy of the plateau, let us briefly sum up its advantages without bestowing indiscreet or over zealous praise. It is pre-eminently a suitable one for the early stages of pulmonary phthsis, especially for such subjects as can and will get out in the air, and are determined to take benefit of the dry, tonic, invigorating, bracing qualities thereof—and keep good hours. Conditions which seem to favor germ propagation and prolong the species of the genus Bacterium do not exist here.

The atmosphere being cool and dry may be called aseptic, though I will not maintain that it will not support bacterial life. Many, or all of you, gentlemen, I dare say, will bear me out that it does not favor such low forms of organic existence.

Wounds heal kindly and operative procedures of the gravest character are rarely followed by septic infection.

The mortality from pulmonary phthisis is not large in any part of North Carolina, being, according to the Mortality Tables of the Tenth Census (1880), 13.4 for every 10,000 of population throughout the State. But it is interesting to note that the mountain counties show a mortality of only 10.6 in every 10,000 of population, as against 16.1 for every 10,000 of population of all the other counties of the State in the aggregate: or in other words, in a State where pulmonary phthisis does not figure prominently in the mortality tables the death rate is still fifty per cent. less in the mountain section than in the other lower-lying portions of the State.

Drs. Avery Segur and T. Mortimer Lloyd, of Brooklyn, made a visit to the plateau in September, 1886, afterward publishing in The New York Medical Journal of April 9, 1887, a very interesting article under the caption, "Some Evidence Relating to Asheville and the Mountains of North Carolina in the Climatic Treatment of Phthisis."

These gentlemen were so well pleased, and so impressed by the apparent climatic advantages of the plateau in the treatment of phthisis, that they instituted a clinical inquiry into its merits "by addressing a circular letter and questions to nearly three hundred prominent physicians in the large cities," many of whom had patients here. I can hardly do better than quote from the "summary of replies" as given in this excellent paper, viz.: "The general opinion is that spring (when mud is gone), summer and autumn months are the most favorable seasons, and that January and February are the most unfavorable months. It is generally agreed that prolonged residence is beneficial. Many recoveries are reported. Dr. Gleitsman gives a striking report of sixty-four cases decidedly improved of eighty-six cases of incipient phthisis. The answers indicate the lasting benefits of an Asheville residence. As would be anticipated the improvement has been chiefly in the early stages, but some striking benefits were experienced in unpromising cases. * * * * All the replies indicate that sleep is favored by this climate. * * * No malaria reported, and the advantages of this region for its treatment indicated."

Among other conditions indicating the advisability of a sojourn in this region may be mentioned asthma, hay fever, convalescence from malarial and other fevers (there are no lakes or swamps and malaria is unknown), nervous prostration and exhaustion from overwork or long continued summer heat; as also chronic congestion of the internal organs, by reason of diminished atmospheric density causing a determination of blood to the surface, hence the great benefit of altitude in incipient phthisis. Nervous energy and muscular vigor are usually increased, and the nutrition of the body and the condition of the blood improved by a sojourn at moderate elevation; above 6,000 feet the appetite for food is diminished and the digestive organs

frequently disordered, whereas a medium altitude usually in
creases the desire for food and quickens digestion. By reason
of its medium altitude contra-indications to a residence upon
the plateau are few, though organic disease of the heart where
the circulation is much disturbed must not be lost sight of. Of
course those who are in advanced phthisis and are too feeble to
breathe the out-of-door air, and take some sort of out-of-door
exercise, are better off at home with their friends, surrounded by
comforts that cannot be supplied elsewhere.

SUMMARY OF METEOROLOGICAL OBSERVATIONS OF THE WINTER OF 1888-1889,

MADE AT

THE U. S. SIGNAL SERVICE STATION, WINYAH SANITARIUM. ASHEVILLE, N. C.

Elevation, 2,350 feet above Sea Level. Latitude, 35.36 N. Longitude, 82.28 W. (Hours of observation, 7 A. M., 2 P. M., and 9 P. M.)

(Self registered max. and min. thermometer with Northern exposure of all instruments, protected from direct rays and radiation from the sun. Barometer correction for altitude averages about 2½ inches. The readings given are reduced to the sea level).

MONTH.	Mean Temperature.	Mean Maximum Temp.	Mean Minimum Temp.	Absolute Maximum Temp.	Absolute Minimum Temp.	Mean Daily Range of Temperature.	Mean Relative Humidity.	Mean Absolute Humidity.	Number of Clear and Fair days.	Number of Cloudy and Rainy Days.	Number of Days Without Sunshine.	Number of Days on which 0.01 or more of rain fell.	Total Amount of Rainfall & Melted Snow in Inches.	Snowfall in Inches	Number of Days on which 0.10 or more of snow fell.	Mean Barometer Corrected for Altitude and Temp.	Direction of Prevailing Winds.	Mean Force of Wind on Scale of 0 to 6.
November	48 40	60 12	40 96	69 50	28 40	19 16	64 20	2 214	23	7	2	7	3 49	0	0	30 18	NW	1 88
December	41 50	54 10	36 68	62 40	22 10	17 44	62 80	2 014	25	5	2		2 94	0	0	30 20	NW	1 40
January	38 50	48 00	29 30	59 80	13 00	18 70	66 30	1 966	24	6	2	9	2 50	0 20	1	30 21	N&NW	0 94
February	37 00	46 73	26 00	69 50	6 0	20 73	55 60	1 894	24	4	1	4	1 08	4 64	4	30 27	N&NW	1 18
March	45 00	55 44	35 72	72 80	21 30	19 72	58 40	2 120	26	5	0	7	0 43	0	0	30 16	N&NW	1 06
April	56 38	67 74	44 12	83 00	29 50	22 66	53 44	2 751	25	5	0	7	1 45	0	0	30 08	N&NW	1 90
Total	266 78	332 13	212 76	417 00	120 10	118 37	360 74	13 062	147	32	6	27	12 58	4 74	5	181 10		8 36
Mean for winter months	44 46	55 35	35 46	69 50	20 20	19 73	60 12	2 177	24 5	5 3	1	1 65	2 09	......	......	30 18	NW	1 39

KARL von RUCK, M. D., OBSERVER.

SUMMARY OF METEOROLOGICAL OBSERVATIONS

MADE AT

THE UNITED STATES SIGNAL SERVICE STATION, WINYAH SANITARIUM, ASHEVILLE, N. C.

Elevation above Sea, 2,350 feet.   Latitude 35.36 N.   Longitude 82.26 W.   Hours of Observation, 7 A. M., 2 P. M., and 9 P. M.

Self registering maximum and minimum thermometers. Instruments exposed in standard U. S. Signal Service Shelter. Barometric reductions for altitude and temperature at 32° F averages about 2.5 inches. Ozone observations after method of Negretti and Zambra.

SEASON.	MONTH.	Mean Temperature.	Mean Max. Temp.	Absolute Max. Temp.	Mean Min. Temp.	Absolute Min. Temp.	Mean Daily Range Temp.	Mean Daily Variation Temp.	Mean Relative Humidity.	Mean Absolute Humidity. (Grs. Moist. per cu. ft. air.)	Mean Barometer corrected for Altitude and Temp.	Mean Amount Ozone (per ct. of possible 100.)	Total Amount of Rain and Melted Snow in Inches.	No. Days on which 00.1 or more rain fell.	Snow Fall in Inches.	No. Clear and Fair Days.	No. Cloudy and Hazy Days.	No. Days without Sunshine.
Summer of 1880.	May	62 44	73 39	83 00	52 13	36 40	21 26	3 07	61 85	39 11	30 07	40 45	4 44	15		29	2	
	June	71 68	83 19	90 00	61 18	53 50	22 01	2 00	71 94	61 57	30 10	30 61	1 18	8		29	1	
	July	70 78	81 09	88 50	62 23	55 00	18 76	2 51	72 85	58 60	30 14	31 61	5 95	15		21	3	
	August	65 91	78 31	86 00	59 20	47 00	19 02	2 48	72 34	54 62	30 17	34 80	6 71	18		27	4	2
	September	65 53	76 14	80 00	44 44	29 50	17 91	2 45	77 22	54 67	30 13	38 50	3 86	16		25	5	2
	October	53 09	63 88	80 00	44 44	29 50	19 44	4 01	70 22	33 07	30 13	53 71	3 77	9	1	28	3	3
	Sums	391 43	456 0	513 80	50 287	20 271	118 40	16 72	436 03	301 64	180 78	241 57	25 77	80	1	159	18	7
	Means	65 24	76 08	85 63	56 25	45 20	19 73	2 79	71 00	50 27	30 13	40 26	4 29	13 33		27 07	31 16	16

KARL von RUCK, B. S., M. D., DIRECTOR OF OBSERVATORY.

C. P. AMBLER, OBSERVER.

SUMMARY OF METEOROLOGICAL OBSERVATIONS

MADE AT

THE UNITED STATES SIGNAL SERVICE STATION, WINYAH SANITARIUM, ASHEVILLE, N. C.

Elevation above S: a, 2,350 feet.   Latitude 35.36 N.   Longitude 82.36 W.   Hours of Observation, 7 A. M., 2 P. M., and 9 P. M.

Self-registering maximum and minimum thermometers. Instruments exposed in standard U. S. Signal Service Shelter. Barometric reductions for altitude and temperature at 32° F averages about 2.5 inches. Ozone observations after method of Negretti and Zambra.

SEASON	MONTH	Mean Temperature	Mean Max. Temperature	Absolute Max. Temp.	Mean Min. Temp.	Absolute Min. Temp.	Mean Daily Range Temp.	Mean Daily Variation Temp.	Mean Relative Humidity	Mean Absolute Humidity (Grs. Mist. per cu. ft. air.)	Mean Barometer Corrected for Altitude and Temp.	Mean Amount Ozone (per ct of possible 100)	Total Amount of Rain and Melted Snow in Inches	No days on which 0.1 or more rain fell	Snow Fall in Inches	No. Clear and Fair Days	No. Cloudy and Rainy Days	No. Days without Sunshine
	November	51.39	65.01	80	38.54	22.5	26.47	4.06	54.21	2.495	30.21	45.88	0.20	3	0	26	22	0
	December	39.23	51.10	64	28.00	16.5	22.50	6.06	64.43	1.821	30.22	27.25	2.44	8	7.80	21	10	1
	January	37.57	45.78	68	28.84	14.0	16.34	5.18	65.74	1.798	30.21	40.10	4.45	13	1.90	22	16	0
Winter of 1890–1891.	February	45.10	53.87	69	36.14	14	16.91	1.77	69.02	2.606	30.19	5.87	8.65	17	1.20	13	15	4
	March	41.83	51.14	69	34.23	14	17.73	5.94	70.93	2.86	30.15	78.06	6.54	18	2.5	20	11	2
	April	56.99	68.51	83	45.64	2.8	20.87	4.36	59.08	3.046	30.15	68.17	1.81	8		25		2
	Total	271.11	333.41	436	211.99	107.9	121.42	33.715	380	34.026	181.13	265.34	23.66	67	15.3	15 3	52	9 9
	Mean for winter months	45.185	55.56	72.68	35.33	17.98	20.23	5.62	63	5.771	30.18	44.22	3.94	11.1	2.55	2 65	8	5

KARL von RUCK, B. S., M. D., DIRECTOR OF OBSERVATORY.   C. P. AMBLER, M. D., OBSERVER.

MEAN TEMPERATURE (DEGREES FAHR.) OBSERVED AT ASHEVILLE, N. N. C., BY W. W. MCDOWELL, F. J KRON, E. J. ASTON, DR. W. ZLEITZMAN, DR. B. H. DOUGLASS, AND KARL VON RUCK, VOLUNTARY OBSERVERS.

Year.	January.	February.	March.	April.	May.	June.	July.	August.	September.	October.	November.	December.	Annual.
1857								70.0	64.4			41.8	
1858	39.1	33 7	42.0	52.2	61.1	69.8							
1867					61.7	69.0	72.4	69.8	67.7	53.6	47.6	40.7	
1868	33.2	36.3	48.7	52.9	60.7	68 2	73.4	70.6	66.0	55.1	42.2	33.2	53.4
1869	42.1	39.9	43.6	53.4	59.4	67.4	71.2	71.8	62.5	48.6	40.5	37.2	53.1
1870	41.3	38.6	41.7	53.7	62.2	67.8	73.2	71.8	64.0	54.8	44.4	33.8	53.9
1871	34.9	43.8	50.8	58.0	62.1	70.8	70.6	72.4	61.4		46.0	37.4	
1872	33.8	38.2	39.4	56.9	64.2	68.4	73.0	71.1	63.7	53.5	40.3	35.0	53.1
1873	35.0	40.5	42.4	53.5	62.7	68.8	71.5	70.8	64.6	50.5	41.7	38.9	53.2
1874	39.7	40.8	52.1	51.2	65.0	71.2	72.8	69.9	66.4	53.5	45.0	41.0	55.7
1875	36.5	34.3	39.8	48.0	62.0	67.3	71.8	68.8	60 8	49.0	48.3	43.2	52.5
1876	42.7	40.5	44.4	58.1	72.3	76.8	72.9	71.9	64 0	52.3	43 1	29.8	55.7
1877	40.1	42.3	44.4	59.8	60.0	69.5	72.7	70.0	64.2	55.2	45.1	42 0	55.4
1878	34.0	39.4	50.9	50.9			74.7	72.5	64.7				
1879	35.9	36.1	48.7		64.0			67.6	61.3	59.9		44.8	
1880	46.4	42.6	47.6										
1884											46.0	41.0	
1885	36.0			51.0	60.0					83.0	44 0		
1887		49 3											
1888	39.6												
1889	38.8	36 3	45.4	56.4	62.6	67.2	72.9	68.8	63.9	52.3	45.3	51 2	55.1
1890	47.2	49.0	42.6	56.8	62.4	71.7	70.8	67.9	65.6	53 0	51.4	39.2	56.5
Mean	38.9	40.1	45.3	54.2	62.6	69.6	72.4	70.4	64.1	55.3	44.7	39.3	54.3

ELEVATED HEALTH STATIONS ABOUT THE PLATEAU.

The point which would at first appeal to the writer as *par excellence* the most eligible as an elevated sanitary station, leaving out of account the fact that as yet human habitation does not invite the invalid, is Craggy, a spur of the grand old Blue Ridge, where, but eighteen miles to the eastward of Asheville, several hundred acres of almost level land lie *perdu* for enterprise and capital presently to make blossom like the rose, and ring with the joyous shouts of convalescence. The altitude of this intoxicating plateau is in the neighborhood of six thousand feet, and its meteorological conditions can hardly be misjudged with our knowledge of our own immediate influences. With no flies or mosquitoes, plenty of sunshine, cold, crystal-like free-stone water, with a summer temperature of from 65 to 68, with scenic surroundings which beggar description, what more can be asked? And this all but an annex of Asheville! Already steam and electricity, without special aim, are making for this point, soon to become famous. It does not require the gift of prophecy to foresee summer and even winter camps dotting our mountain slopes from Morganton in Burke, to Murphy in Cherokee. Truly, over the Adirondacks the advantages are manifest. Gladly will we relinquish to the Adirondacks her beautiful lakes for a surcease of insect life and exemption from even the possibilities of miasmatic infection. Our streams are as full of trout, our woods as full of game: nor have we the ruggedness of winter, nor the cold, damp nights of summer, nor yet the amount of rain in either season. As a further exemption, without statistics to bear me out, I make bold to say that hay fever sufferers will here enjoy an immunity, almost complete if not quite, from that dread malady.

The Sparkling Catawba Springs are 6 miles from Hickory, in Catawba county, on W. N. C. R. R., and are 1,200 feet high. Mean temperature 56°. Blue and white sulphur and chalybeate water. Hotel capacity, 300.

Between Hickory and Lenoir is beautiful Highbriten, a cone shaped mountain in the Bushy mountains 2.242 feet high, with a good road winding around from its base to its top.

Thirty-five miles from Marion are Linville Falls and about the same distance from Johnson City, Tenn. Along the upper

Linville River, and at base of Grandfather Mountain, is a table land where there is situate Linville and a good hotel. Elevation of the Eseeola Inn at Linville 3,800 feet, reached most easily via Johnson City, Tenn.

Glen Alpine Springs in Burke county, 13 miles from Morganton, 10 miles from Bridgewater, on W. N. C. R. R., are 1,500 feet high. Sulphur and chalybeate water and a hotel with 200 capacity.

Blowing Rock is on the top of the Blue Ridge Mountains, about 15 miles west of Lenoir, the county seat of Caldwell county and the terminus of the Chester and Lenoir Narrow Guage Railroad. It also is on a plateau or table land, varying in width from three to five miles. It is in Wautauga county, and the highest incorporated town east of the Rocky Mountains, being 4,090 feet above sea level. About two miles off is the Wautauga Falls, and towards the Johns River valley is another beautiful fall, the name of which I have forgotten. There are splendid drives along the crest of the Blue Ridge, along the Wautanga River and through Valle Crucis, where Bishop Ives founded a Mission long before the war, and where our Rev. Dr. Buxton began his life as a clergyman. A friend, after speaking of the obliteration of all traces of the good Bishop's work, uses this language, " But the valley keeps its shape and the cross, on which his Master died, remains forever outlined there." Blowing Rock Gap is 3,779 feet high ; mean temperature, 48.7. Boone, the county seat of Wautauga, is eight miles west, and is 3,242 feet high. Visible from Blowing Rock, are Hawks Bill, 4,090 feet, Table Rock, 3,918 feet, and the Grandfather Mountain, which, at its top, shows rocks of the oldest geological formation on the earth's surface. It is 5,897 feet high. From it a magnificent view of the surrounding country can be had. Even Kings Mountain in South Carolina is plainly visible. It is only ten miles from Blowing Rock to the top of the Grandfather. A good farm house at the base affords a comfortable night's lodging, and the ascent and descent may be made from this house in a day, leaving a long time for a view on the top at mid-day. Near the top, on the

Elk River side of the mountain, is said to be one of the coldes springs known.

Marion is the county seat of McDowell county, on the W. N. C. R. R., and thirty miles north of it is Bakersville, the county seat of Mitchell county, and eight miles northwest from it is the Roan Mountain, the most beautiful mountain of the entire North Carolina system. On the top of this mountain 6,306 feet high, is a comfortable hotel, capable of accommodating 75 people. Here sufferers from hay fever find relief. The view is simply grand. It is about ten miles from Cranberry Iron Mines, one of the richest mines in the world, to which point a railroad runs from Johnson City, Tenn.

Piedmont Springs is fifteen miles from Morganton. Sulphur and chalybeate water.

Round Knob, in McDowell county, near top of the Blue Ridge, 2,000 feet high, on W. N. C. R. R., has a hotel and, near by, fine lithia water.

Waynesville, in Haywood county, is thirty miles west of Asheville, on Ducktown branch of W. N. C. R. R., and is 2,756 feet high. White Sulphur Springs, one-half mile away, has a good hotel.

Hendersonville is 2,167 feet high and is twenty miles south of Asheville, on Asheville and Spartanburg Railroad. Temperature 55.5. It has hotels, good water and broad, well-shaded streets.

Flat Rock is three miles south, with a hotel, and around it are clustered many fine residences.

Cæsar's Head is a mountain peak 20 miles from Hendersonville and 24 miles from Greenville, S. C. It is 3,225 feet high. On the road you pass the grand Buck Forest and the exquisite falls of the Little River.

Highlands, in Macon county, is situated on the crest of the Blue Ridge, near the intersection of North and South Carolina and Georgia, 21 miles east of Franklin, Macon county, N. C., which latter place is 20 miles from Webster, on the line of the W. N. C. R. R. It is about 40 miles from Webster, over the Cowee and Culowhee Mountains. It is a table-land on the top of the Blue Ridge, about two miles wide on the average, sloping gently towards the West. It is 4,000 feet above tide water. It is 150 feet below the crest of the Blue Ridge and about three-quarters of a mile from the gap of the mountain. From Satoola (Stooly), a mountain south of the village, easily reached by a gentle climb of 1½ miles, a splendid view of Whitesides, Fodder stack, Black Rock, Chimney Top, the Balsams, Cowee, Nanta-hala and Smoky Mountains, can be obtained, while far in the dim distance, through a gap in the Nantahala Range, Lookout Mountain in Tennessee towers up, so shadowy and impalpable that it seems you could cut it with a paper knife. There are well graded roads in the vicinity, while two miles to the west, a little off the main road, is the Dry Falls of the Cullasagee, or the Pitcher Falls of the Sugar Fork of the Little Tennessee River, by both of which names a picturesque water fall is known. The creek leaps from a high rock to a ledge sixty feet below, under which you can pass dry shod. From the ledge the creek takes a second plunge some forty feet lower down, and then hurries on to the valley. In the Whitesides Mountain is the famous Devil's Pulpit.

From all that the writer can learn Highlands must enjoy exceptional climatic advantages. It has a splendid altitude, and is sheltered from the winds to the north and east by the crest of the Blue Ridge. It is one of the loftiest settlements east of the Rocky Mountains. I cannot pass it by without the prediction of a brilliant future in the world of resorts.

The temperature record shows spring 52, summer 68, autumn 53, winter 30, year 50. It appears to be dryer than the Roan, but effort to obtain accurate statistics for humidity and rainfall has been fruitless. Visitors and health-seekers are enchanted. The soil is light, sandy, and seems as greedy of moisture as the air itself.

This desirable point may be reached via Sylva, a station of the Western North Carolina Railroad, from which point it is 40 miles distant.

The Roan Mountain, in Mitchell County, stands pre-eminent as one of the most interesting mountains in the Appalachian system. It rears its bared head 6,300 feet above the sea, and the views and cloud effects are marvelous. No less so are the acres upon acres of rhododendrons, which are in the glory of their bloom from the 15th to 20th of June. A good hotel, the Cloudland, fitting the situation, graces the summit. This interesting point may be reached via Johnson City, Tenn., and the narrow guage to Roan Mountain Station, thence 14 miles by stage to the top. This is the Mecca of the hay fever sufferer, but will prove too damp for the phthisical.

Hot Springs, in Madison county, altitude 1,326 feet, with hot springs of about 100° of heat, are too well known to call for extended notice in the limits of such a paper.

Tryon City, in Polk county, famous as being in the thermal belt, altitude 1,500 feet, is indeed a point worthy of attention. That its climato-therapeutic advantages are pronounced ; is abundantly established by patients who have derived great benefit from a residence there. This so-called thermal belt is about five miles long by three-quarters wide, where the meteorological conditions are so modified by its southern slope and mountain barriers on the north, and differ so much from the circumjacent territory that the effect upon vegetation is startling.

It would appear from the foregoing epitome of our unique geographical and meteorological situation, that by some conjoint action of the medical profession and the intelligent co-operation of capital and enterprise, there might be established with us, and round about us, between Salisbury and Murphy, a series of sanitaria at elevations varying from 1,200 to 6,000 feet, which would prove advantageous to each other and of immeasurable benefit to the community at large. For example, I would suggest as stations, 1st, Tryon City, in Polk county, with its 1,500 feet and its thermal belt ; 2d, Asheville, as the central and most important station, and 3d, Craggy, with its 6,000 feet, as the crowning eyrie of all.